The UPs and DOWNs of GRAVITY

DAVID A. ADLER

ILLUSTRATED BY ANNA RAFF

HOLIDAY HOUSE NEW YORK

What happens to a ball when it falls off a table?

It falls to the floor.

Why doesn't it keep rolling straight ahead, suspended in air, or fly up off the table?

The answer is **GRAVITY**.

Gravity is what makes snowflakes fall to the ground. It's what keeps your chair from floating off the floor. It's why no matter how high and how hard you throw a football it comes down, hopefully so someone can catch it.

Sir Isaac Newton, an English scientist and philosopher who lived from 1642 to 1727, was the first to describe gravity. It is said that his interest began one summer day when he saw an apple fall from a tree. Why did the apple fall, Newton wondered, instead of just floating off? According to some reports, Newton noticed the fall of the apple accelerated (fell more quickly), as it got closer to the ground. That meant some force must be pulling the apple toward the ground. That force was gravity.

Gravity is an invisible force that pulls one object to another. The strength of the pull depends on two things:
1. the mass of the two objects
2. how close they are to each other

The greater the mass of the two objects and the closer they are to each other, the greater the gravitational pull.

What is **MASS**? It's the measure of how much matter is in something. A marshmallow and a chocolate bar are different forms of **MATTER**. They can be the same size, but they don't have the same mass.

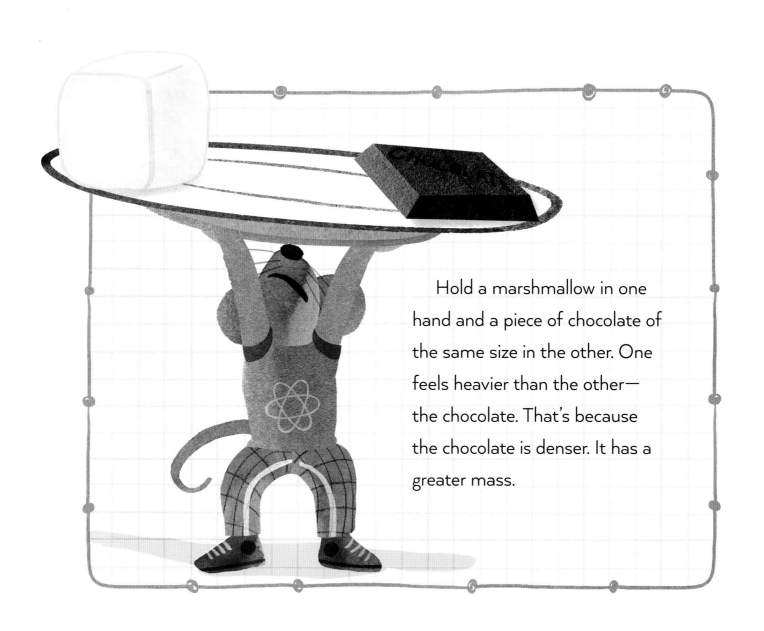

Hold a marshmallow in one hand and a piece of chocolate of the same size in the other. One feels heavier than the other—the chocolate. That's because the chocolate is denser. It has a greater mass.

When you jump, two objects pull on each other: you and the planet Earth. Of course, Earth is much larger than you are, so its pull is much greater than yours. The greater gravitational pull of the planet is the reason why you come down when you jump up.

The **WEIGHT** of an object depends on the strength of the pull of gravity.

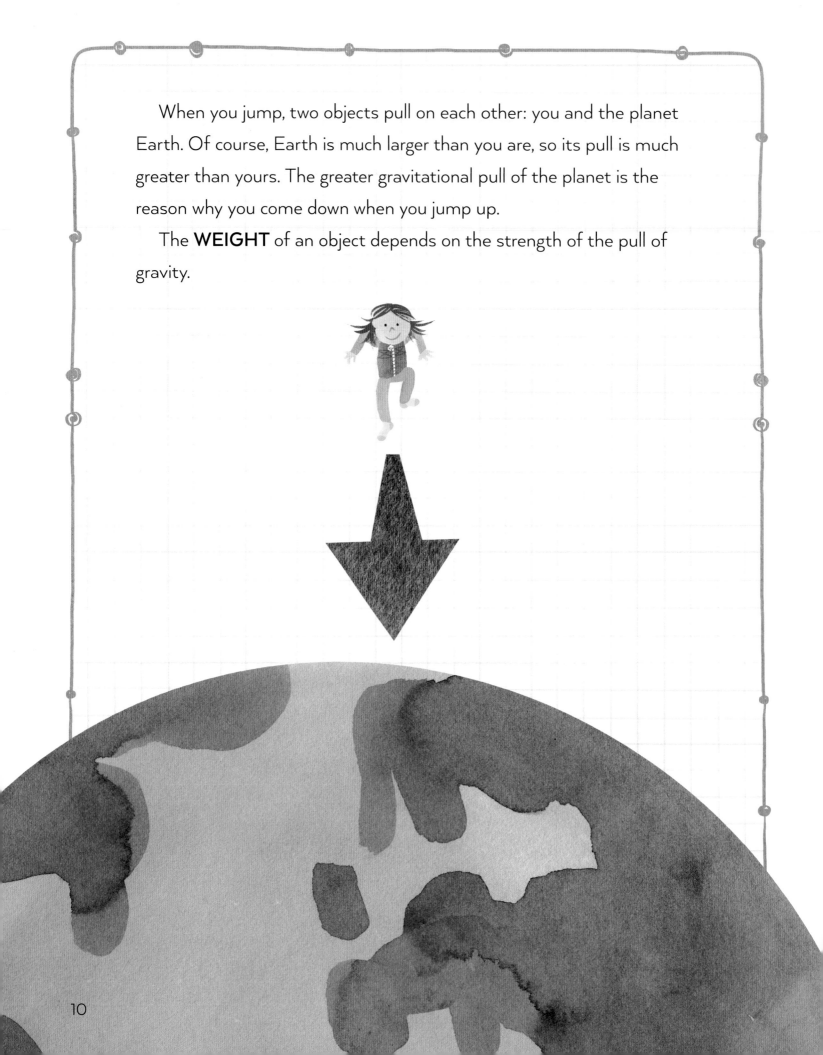

When you weigh an apple, you are measuring the gravitational pull on the apple. The pull is determined by the mass of two objects, the apple and the planet Earth, and on how close they are to each other.

As long as the size and density of an object does not change, its mass does not change. But an object's weight can change.

What if the apple was on the moon? The moon's mass is much less than Earth's, so its gravitational pull is less. An apple weighs less on the moon than it does on Earth.

An apple that weighs 6 ounces (170 grams) on Earth would weigh about 1 ounce (28 grams) on the moon.

The apple's mass has not changed, but its weight has. Or, more precisely, the gravitational pull on the apple has changed.

MOON

MARS

EARTH

VENUS

MERCURY

JUPITER
SATURN
URANUS
NEPTUNE
PLUTO

The sun, the moon, and the planets each have their own gravitational pull. The larger and denser the planet, the sun, or the moon, the greater its gravitational pull.

If you weigh 100 pounds (45 kilograms) on Earth, your weight on the moon would be 16 pounds (7 kilograms). Your mass wouldn't change, but the gravitational pull on you would.

The planet Jupiter is about 11 times bigger than Earth. It has a much greater mass, so its gravitational pull is stronger. If you weigh 100 pounds (45 kilograms) on Earth, your weight on Jupiter would be 252 pounds (114 kilograms).

EARTH
100 lbs.
(45 Kg)

JUPITER
252 lbs.
(114 Kg)

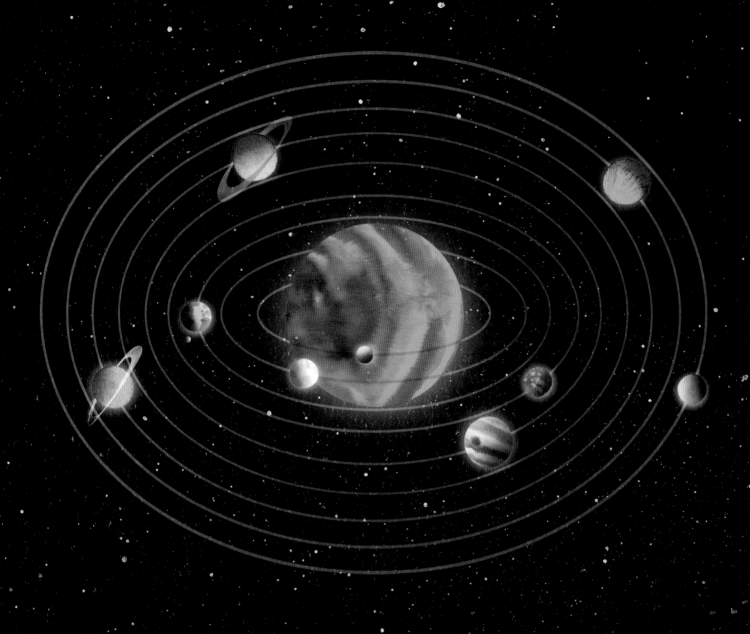

The sun's mass is more than 300,000 times greater than Earth's, so of course its gravitational pull is much greater. If you weigh 100 pounds on Earth, your weight on the sun would be 2,800 pounds (1,270 kilograms). Again, your mass hasn't changed, but the gravitational pull on you has.

The gravitational pull of the much-larger sun keeps Earth and other planets in their orbits. Without the sun, Earth and the other planets in the solar system would fly off into space.

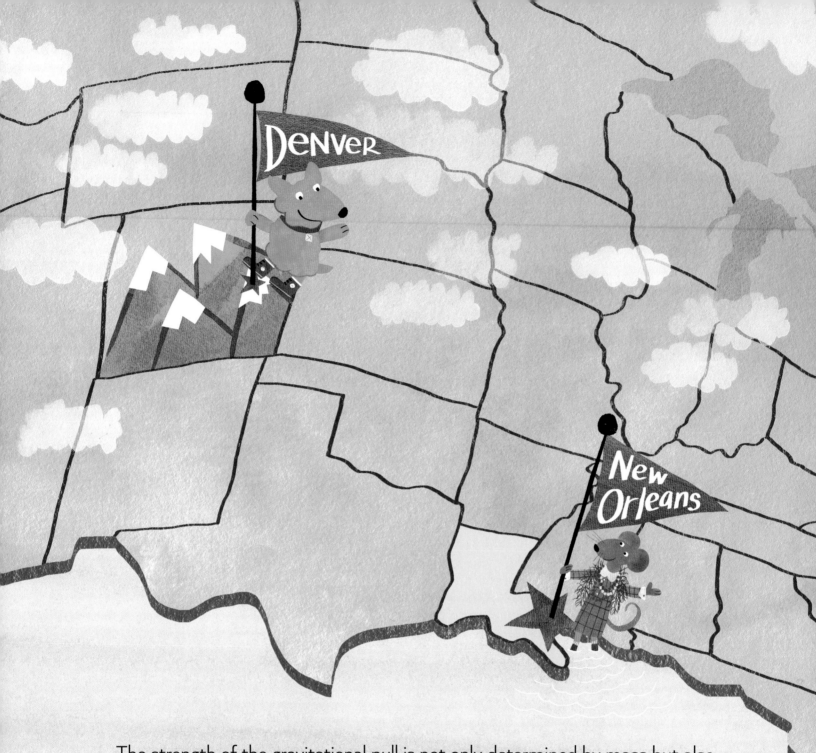

The strength of the gravitational pull is not only determined by mass but also by distance. The closer two objects are, the stronger the gravitational pull. This explains why we would weigh slightly less in Denver, Colorado (the Mile High City), than we would in a sea-level city such as New Orleans, Louisiana. That's because Denver is at a higher altitude and is therefore farther away from the center of Earth.

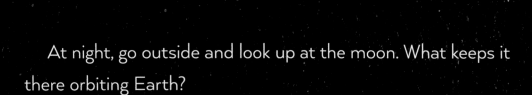

At night, go outside and look up at the moon. What keeps it there orbiting Earth?

Gravity.

The gravitational pull of the much-larger Earth keeps the moon in its **ORBIT**. Without that pull, the moon would fly off into space.

Why doesn't Earth's gravity pull the moon to Earth?

Inertia.

Sir Isaac Newton explained **INERTIA**. Inertia means that matter that is moving tends to keep moving, and matter at rest tends to remain at rest.

If you have ever been in a car when it makes a quick stop, you may have felt the power of inertia. Do you remember lurching forward? Do you remember your seat belt saving you from hitting the back of the seat in front of you? The car stopped, but you didn't. Inertia kept you moving forward.

With a spoon, try stirring a cup of water. Then stop. You've taken the spoon out of the water, but because of inertia the water keeps spinning.

21

The moon's gravitational pull is much weaker than Earth's, but it still affects Earth. Sit on a beach at the edge of an ocean, and you'll see its effect on water. At high tide the water covers more of the beach than it does at low tide. High and low tides, the rise and fall of the ocean, are caused by the moon's gravitational pull.

The pull of gravity is nearly the same for all things, even things with different masses. You can prove it.

Drop a Ping-Pong ball and a baseball at the same time. They will hit the ground together.

Then drop a baseball and a feather at the same time. They won't hit the ground together, but not because the pull of gravity is different for the baseball and the feather. The ball and the feather are not falling through empty space. They are falling through air. The air interferes with the pull of gravity. Because the feather is larger and lighter, air resistance has a greater effect on it than on the ball.

DEMONSTRATING RESISTANCE IN FALLING OBJECTS

This experiment will help explain what happened with the baseball and the feather.

YOU WILL NEED:

- a marble
- a large pot
- water

Drop the marble in the empty pot. It very quickly hits the bottom of the pot.

Fill the pot almost to the top with water, then drop the marble in. This time the fall takes a bit longer.

The water interfered with the pull of gravity. That's what happened with the baseball and the feather. The air interfered with their fall.

DEMONSTRATING AIR RESISTANCE

Take two same-sized sheets of paper. Crush one into a ball. The papers weigh the same, but the balled-up paper has a smaller surface area. Drop both at the same time. The balled-up paper will land first. Air resistance is greater for the flat sheet of paper than it is for the balled-up paper. The air resistance was greater for the feather than for the baseball.

Something falling with only gravity pulling it down, with absolutely no air resistance is said to be "free falling." Free-falling objects all fall at the same rate, and astronaut David R. Scott proved it.

Scott was the commander of the 1971 Apollo 15 mission. He stood on the surface of the moon, pretty much an air-free environment, and at the same time dropped a hammer and a feather. The hammer weighed almost 3 pounds and the feather just over 1 ounce. The two objects fell at the same rate and hit the surface of the moon at the same time.

There's a lot more to gravity than pulling a ball rolling off a table to the floor, than making snowflakes fall down and not up, than ensuring every time we jump up, we come down. Gravity is a natural force that keeps everything in its place.

GLOSSARY

ACCELERATION – Something increasing its speed.

FREE FALL – Something falling without air resistance.

GRAVITY – The force that attracts one object to another.

INERTIA – Objects on the move tend to continue moving. Those at rest tend to stay at rest.

MASS – The amount of matter, or stuff, in something.

MATTER – Anything that takes up space.

ORBIT – The path of a moon circling a planet and a planet circling the sun.

WEIGHT – The force of gravity pulling on something or someone.

For Hilda Hamada, Happy 100th Birthday —D. A. A.

To Jack and Martha —A.R.

Text copyright © 2020 by David A. Adler

Illustrations copyright © 2020 by Anna Raff

All Rights Reserved

HOLIDAY HOUSE is registered in the U.S. Patent and Trademark Office.

Printed and Bound in September 2020 at Leo Paper, Heshan, China.

The artwork was created with ink washes, assembled and colored digitally.

www.holidayhouse.com

First Edition

1 3 5 7 9 10 8 6 4 2

Library of Congress Cataloging-in-Publication Data

Names: Adler, David A., author. | Raff, Anna, illustrator.

Title: The ups and downs of gravity / by David A. Adler ; illustrated by Anna Raff.

Description: First edition. | New York : Holiday House, 2021.

Audience: Ages 7–10 | Audience: Grades 2–3 | Summary: "Two kids explore the ups
and downs of gravity in this introduction to physical science"—Provided by publisher.

Identifiers: LCCN 2020038383 | ISBN 9780823446360 (hardcover)

Subjects: LCSH: Gravity—Juvenile literature.

Classification: LCC QC178 .A35 2021 | DDC 531/.14—dc23

LC record available at https://lccn.loc.gov/2020038383

ISBN: 978-0-8234-4636-0 (hardcover)